Backyard Animals
Hummingbirds

Edited by Heather C. Hudak

Weigl Publishers Inc.

Published by Weigl Publishers Inc.
350 5th Avenue, Suite 3304, PMB 6G
New York, NY 10118-0069
Website: www.weigl.com

Library of Congress Cataloging-in-Publication Data available upon request.
Fax 1-866-44-WEIGL for the attention of the Publishing Records department.

ISBN 978-1-60596-004-3 (hard cover)
ISBN 978-1-60596-010-4 (soft cover)

Printed in the United States of America
1 2 3 4 5 6 7 8 9 0 12 11 10 09 08

Editor Heather C. Hudak
Design Terry Paulhus

All of the Internet URLs given in the book were valid at the time of publication.
However, due to the dynamic nature of the Internet, some addresses may have
changed, or sites may have ceased to exist since publication. While the author
and publisher regret any inconvenience this may cause readers, no responsibility
for any such changes can be accepted by either the author or the publisher.

Photo Credits

Weigl acknowledges Getty Images as one of its primary image suppliers for this title.

Every reasonable effort has been made to trace ownership and to obtain
permission to reprint copyright material. The publishers would be pleased
to have any errors or omissions brought to their attention so that they may
be corrected in subsequent printings.

Contents

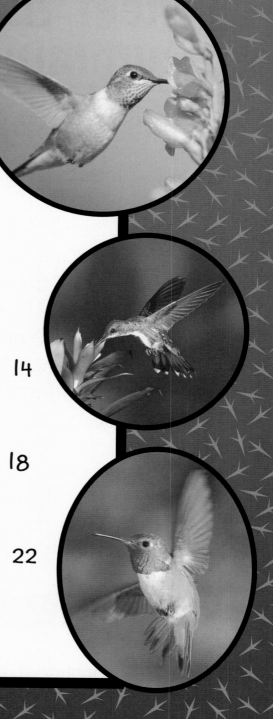

Meet the Hummingbird

Hummingbirds are tiny birds. Like other birds, they lay eggs and have wings and feathers. Hummingbirds can be found in North, Central, and South America.

Hummingbirds come in many sizes, but they are all very small. They range in size from 0.07 ounces (2.2 grams) to 0.7 ounces (20 g).

Hummingbirds can be many colors, including bright greens, blues, reds, and yellows. All hummingbirds have a long **bill**. This helps them to get food from flowers.

Hummingbirds can fly in any direction. They are the only animals that can fly backwards.

Hummingbirds can hover, or hang, in one place for a very long time. This allows them to stay in flight while taking food from flowers.

All about Hummingbirds

There are about 338 known **species** of hummingbird. Most types live in Central and South America. Only 16 types live in North America.

Male and female hummingbirds look different. Males are very colorful, while females are usually more dull. The male hummingbird is usually brighter so that he can attract females.

The black-chinned hummingbird is found in many parts of the western United States.

Where Hummingbirds Live

Allen's
- Lives on the coast of California

Lucifer
- Found in Texas, Arizona, and New Mexico

Ruby-throated
- Found in eastern North America

Calliope
- Lives in the northwestern United States

Hummingbird History

All birds come from a group of dinosaurs called **archosaurs**. Big changes in the environment caused dinosaurs to die out. Birds changed with the environment and developed into many species.

Little is known about how the hummingbird came from other types of birds. Some scientists think that the first hummingbirds developed around 35 million years ago. Others believe that hummingbirds are much more recent.

The first hummingbirds may have come from South America. The largest number of hummingbird species still live there.

Fascinating Facts

There are very few hummingbird **fossils**. This is because hummingbirds have tiny, hollow bones that break easily.

Over time, hummingbirds have developed a long, tube-like beak to suck a sugary liquid called nectar from flowers.

Hummingbird Habitat

Hummingbirds live in places that have warm climates. Most countries in South and Central America have temperatures that are above 70 degrees Fahrenheit (20 degrees Celsius). Hummingbirds that live in North America often **migrate** to South or Central America during the cold winter months.

Most hummingbirds live in forest areas and meadows that have many flowers. They can also be found in cities. Hummingbirds can live anywhere that they find food.

Hummingbirds prefer warmer climates because there is more chance of finding flowers.

Hummingbird nests are the smallest of all birds' nests.

Hummingbird Features

Hummingbirds have many features that help them fly, find food, eat, and survive in nature.

HEAD
Hummingbirds have a large head for their body size. They have the largest brains of all birds in comparison to their size. Hummingbirds are very smart. They can remember places and people for a long time.

FEATHERS
Hummingbirds come in many colors. They can be bright blues and greens, as well as **metallics**.

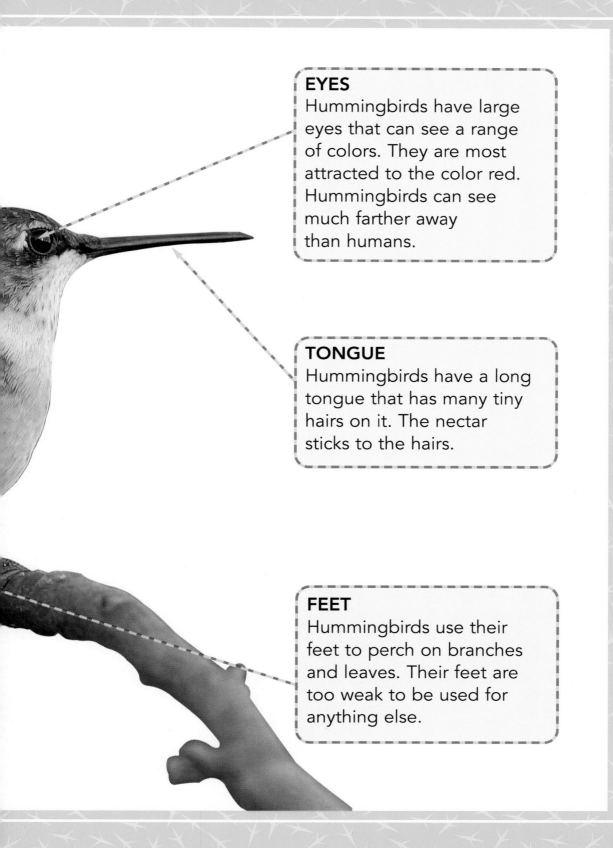

EYES
Hummingbirds have large eyes that can see a range of colors. They are most attracted to the color red. Hummingbirds can see much farther away than humans.

TONGUE
Hummingbirds have a long tongue that has many tiny hairs on it. The nectar sticks to the hairs.

FEET
Hummingbirds use their feet to perch on branches and leaves. Their feet are too weak to be used for anything else.

What Do Hummingbirds Eat?

Hummingbirds spend most of their time flying. They need a great deal of energy to stay in flight. One of the best ways to get energy is from sugar. The nectar of flowers is mostly made up of sugar. Hummingbirds prefer flowers that have bright colors, such as red, orange, and pink.

Hummingbirds also eat small insects, such as gnats, flies, and ants. They find insects on the petals of flowers or in the bark of trees.

Hummingbirds can eat about half of their weight in sugar from nectar each day.

Flies

Flowers

Hummingbirds have many types of food in their diet. They eat insects and nectar from flowers.

Hummingbird Life Cycle

Female hummingbirds make nests on the branches of trees or in shrubs. The mother ties the nest together with silk from spider webs. The silk is sticky and holds the parts of the nest in place.

Eggs

The female hummingbird lays two eggs at a time in her nest. She **incubates** them for about two weeks. The eggs are white in color and about the size of a jellybean.

Nestlings

Baby hummingbirds do not look like adult hummingbirds. They have no feathers, and they cannot move outside of the nest. At this stage, the **nestlings** eat more insects than nectar because the **protein** helps them grow.

It takes working up to five hours each day for a week to build a nest. The nest is about the size of a walnut shell. It can be bigger or smaller depending on the type of hummingbird.

Adults

At about 20 days, young hummingbirds are ready to fly with their mothers. They have feathers and are almost full grown. Once they start flying, most hummingbirds are able to live on their own.

Encountering Hummingbirds

Hummingbirds come to any garden that has flowers with nectar. Brightly colored flowers have a higher chance of attracting hummingbirds.

Some people have special feeders filled with sugary water to encourage hummingbirds to come their gardens. It is best to watch hummingbirds from a distance. They are frightened easily and may fly away if you get too close.

Useful Websites

For more information on hummingbirds, visit **www.hummingbirds.net**.

The length of a hummingbird's bill is half the length of its body.

Myths and Legends

There are many myths and legends about hummingbirds from American Indian cultures. The Hopi Indians believed that hummingbirds could talk to the gods. They would help humans by asking the gods for rain.

Since hummingbirds only live in the Americas, there are no hummingbird myths or legends from other parts of the world.

The Hopi Indians paint hummingbirds on water jars.

The Story of Huitzilopochtli

The Aztecs from Central America had many myths about hummingbirds. The best known myth is about a warrior called Huitzilopochtli, who wore a helmet that was shaped like a hummingbird. Huitzilopochtli was a powerful warrior who fought and won many battles. When he was killed during a legendary battle, his body disappeared into the air. A hummingbird appeared out of the ground where his body had been. The other warriors believed it was Huitzilopochtli. The hummingbird gave them the courage to win the battle.

After this, the Aztecs believed that any warrior who died in battle would become a hummingbird.

Frequently Asked Questions

Do hummingbirds walk?

Answer: Hummingbirds cannot walk because their legs are too small and weak. This is because they spend most of their time flying. The only way hummingbirds use their legs is to perch delicately on branches of trees or plants.

Do hummingbirds live in a group or alone?

Answer: Hummingbirds do not move around in a flock like some other birds. They spend most of their time by themselves. The only time hummingbirds spend together is during the mating season and when a mother is with her nestlings.

Where do hummingbirds get their name from?

Answer: Hummingbirds get their name from the humming noise that is made by the speed of their wings flapping. Their wings have very strong muscles and can flap 15 to 80 times per second.

Puzzler

See if you can answer these questions about hummingbirds.

1. Are male or female hummingbird more brightly colored?
2. How many eggs does a hummingbird lay at one time?
3. At what age are hummingbirds ready to fly?
4. What does the hummingbird eat?
5. How much sugar can a hummingbird eat in one day?

Answers: 1. the male **2.** two **3.** at about 20 days of age **4.** nectar and small insects **5.** half of its body weight

Find Out More

There are many more interesting facts to learn about hummingbirds. Look for these books at your library so you can learn more.

Votaw, Melanie. *Hummingbirds*. Running Press Book Publishers, 2007.

Carroll, Don, and Norito Carrol. *First Flight: Mother Hummingbird's Story*. Andrews McMeel Publishing, 2006.

Words to Know

archosaurs: ancient relatives of birds
bill: the beak of the hummingbird
fossils: the hardened remains of animals or plants that lived long ago
incubates: keeps eggs warm so that the babies inside can grow
metallics: colors that are shiny

migrate: to travel from one country or place to another
nestlings: newborn hummingbirds that live in the nest
protein: a substance found in all living things
species: groups of animals or plants that have many features in common

Index